The more we smile...
The more we seem to shine
The shine glows brighter
The glow sets off a chain reaction
The chain reaction is:
The infectious sparkle and
glimmer of hope we
share with each other.

Copyright © 2021 Missee Nelligan

All rights reserved. No part of this book may be used
or reproduced by any means, graphic, electronic or mechanical,
including photocopying, recording, taping or by any information
storage retrieval system without the written permission of the
author except in the case of brief quotations embodied in
critical articles and reviews.

Blueyesmisty, South Australia, www.blueyesmisty.com
All photos by Tracey-Lee

ISBN: 9798734791332
Imprint: Independently published

One way to fill your heart with joy…
Find something you love to do.

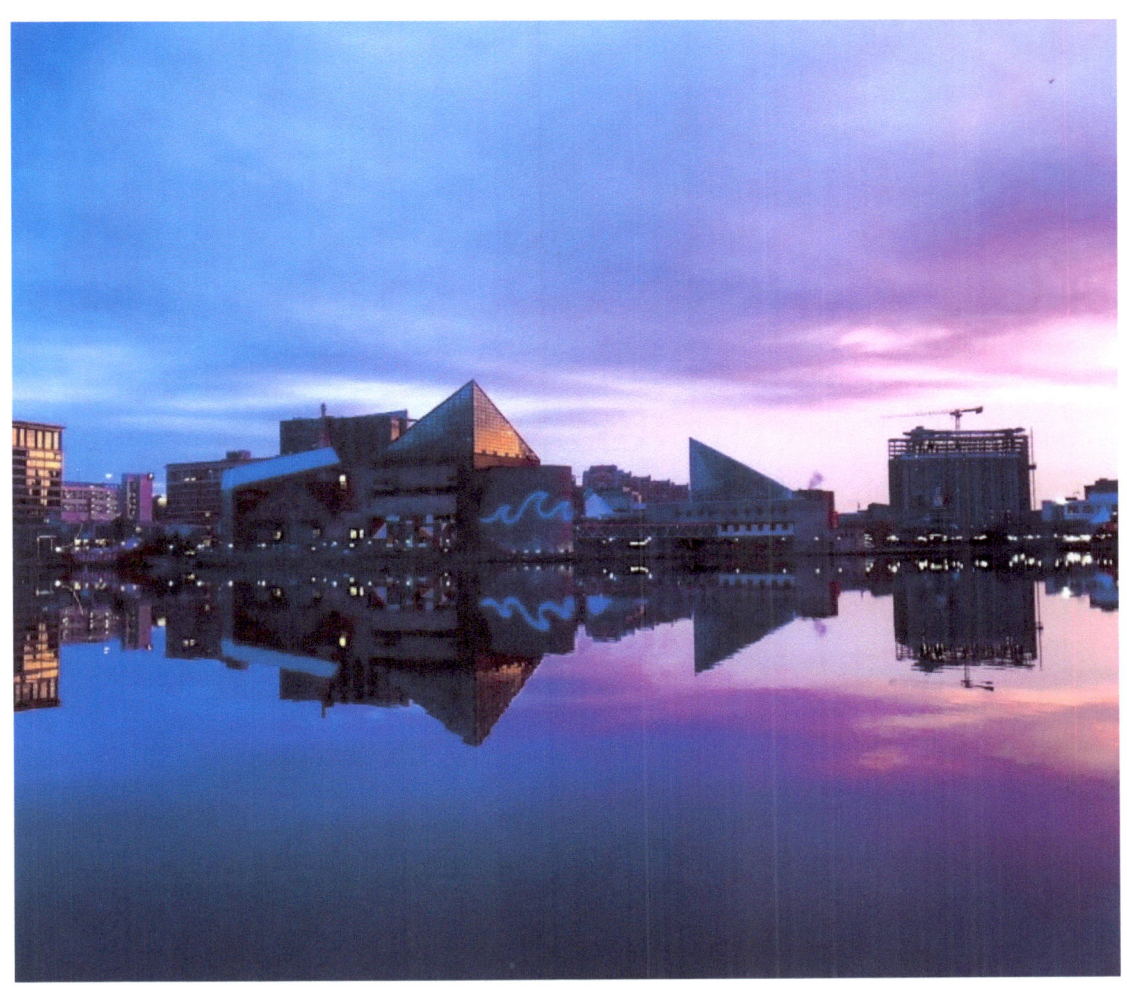

Inner Harbor Baltimore, Maryland United States

You are worthy,
shine everyday.

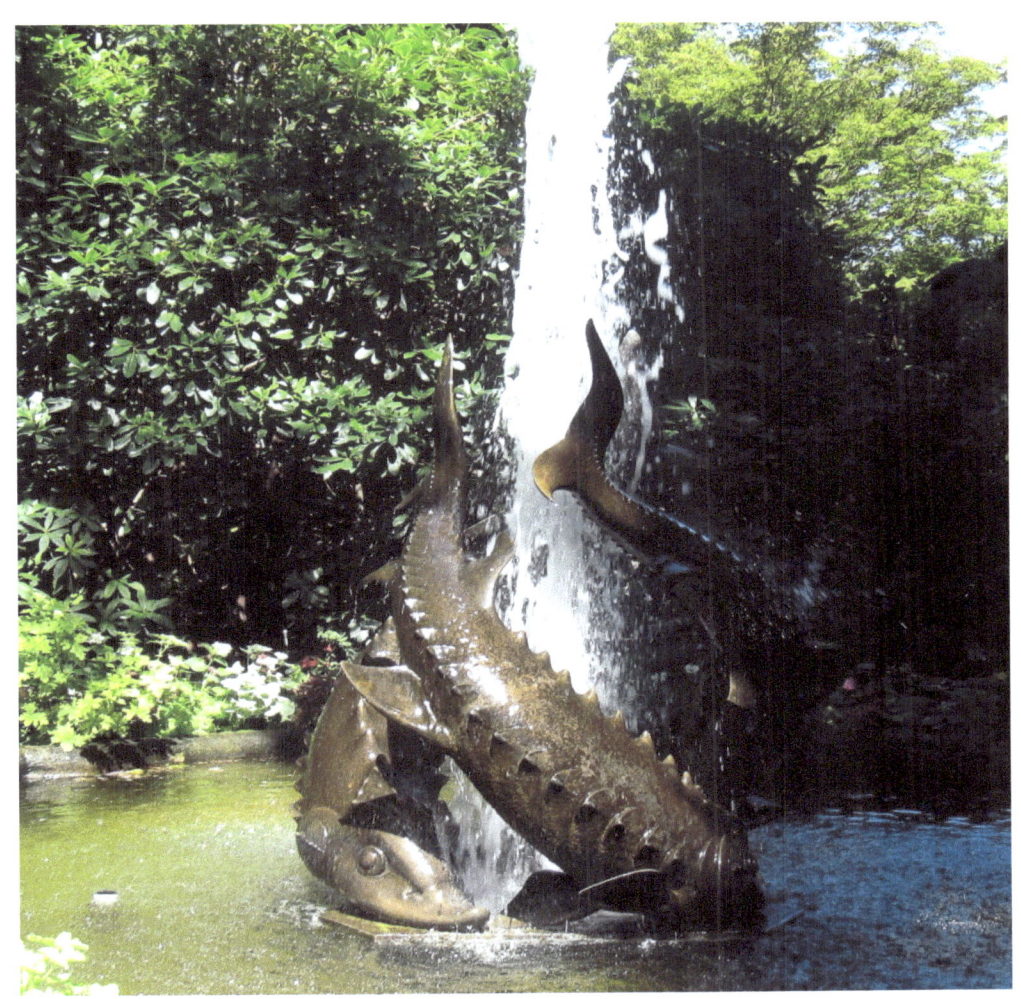

Butchart Gardens, Victoria Canada

Surround yourself with people who make you laugh
when you don't feel like laughing.
Surround yourself with people who encourage
and support you, but also who
love you enough to be honest with you.
Surround yourself with people who will push you
to achieve great things,
because they believe in you.
Surround yourself with people who
love you for you,
who will be there through good times
and bad times.

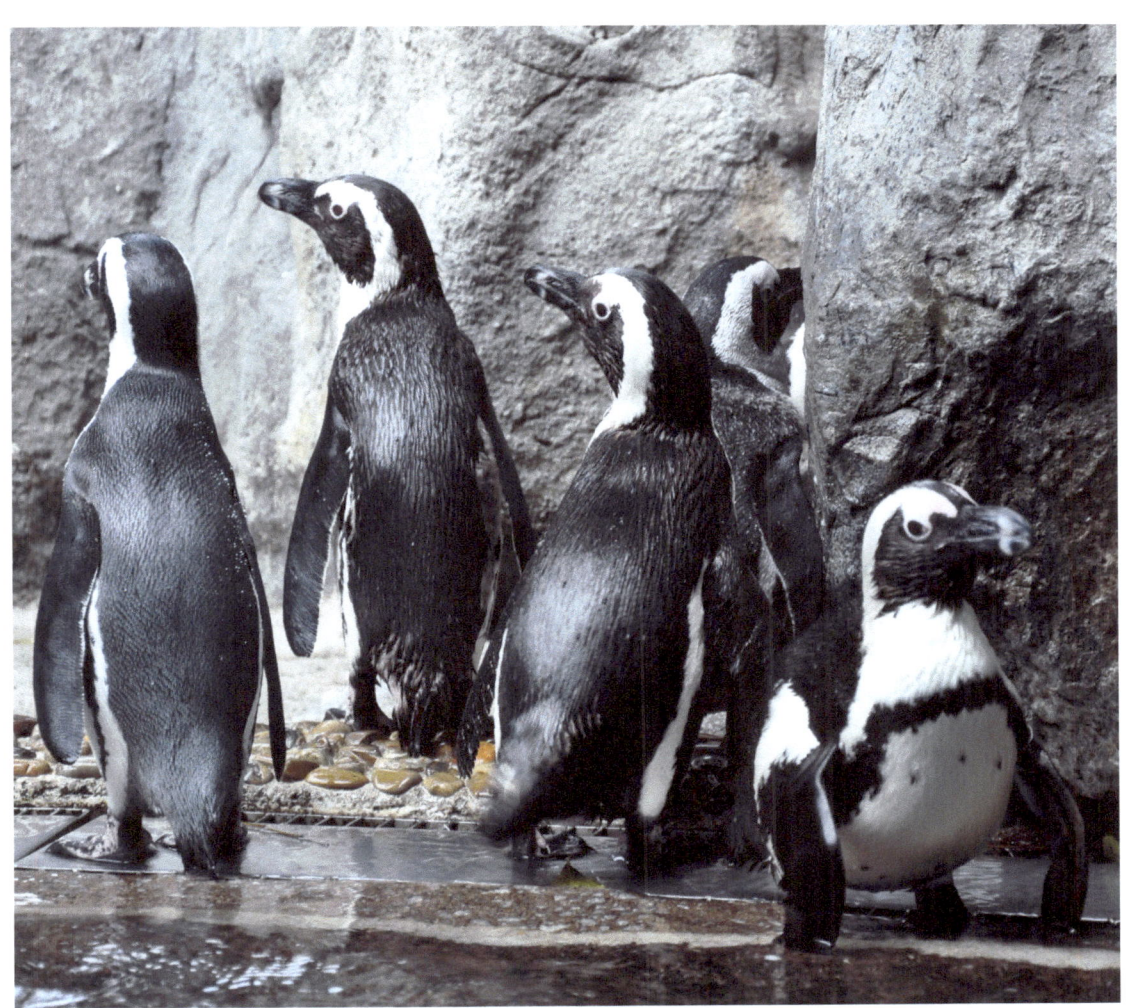
Penguins from the Singapore Zoo

Life will not always
be smooth sailing.
It's how you manoeuvre
the waves of life.

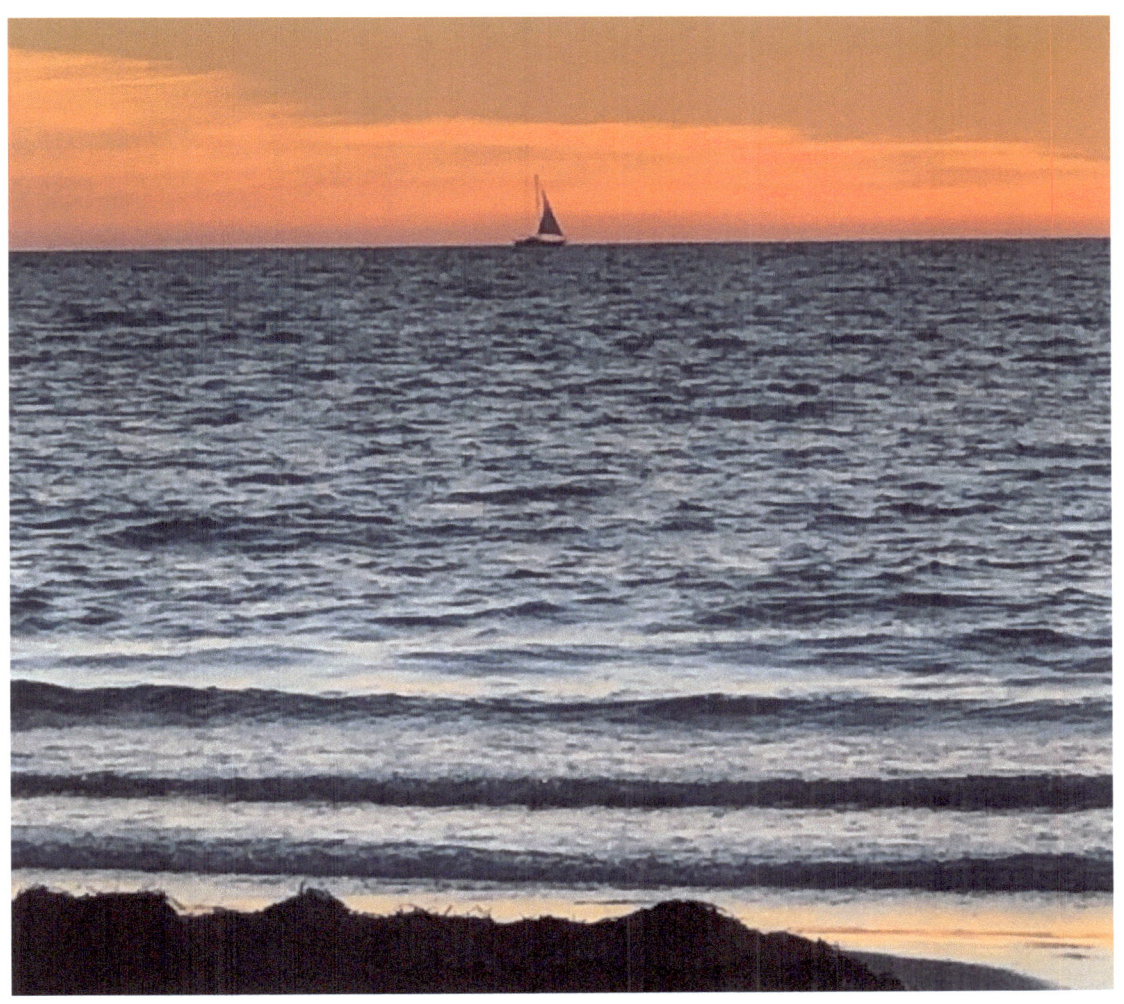

Semaphore Beach, South Australia

There is always
a beginning...
There is a middle...
There certainly is
an end.

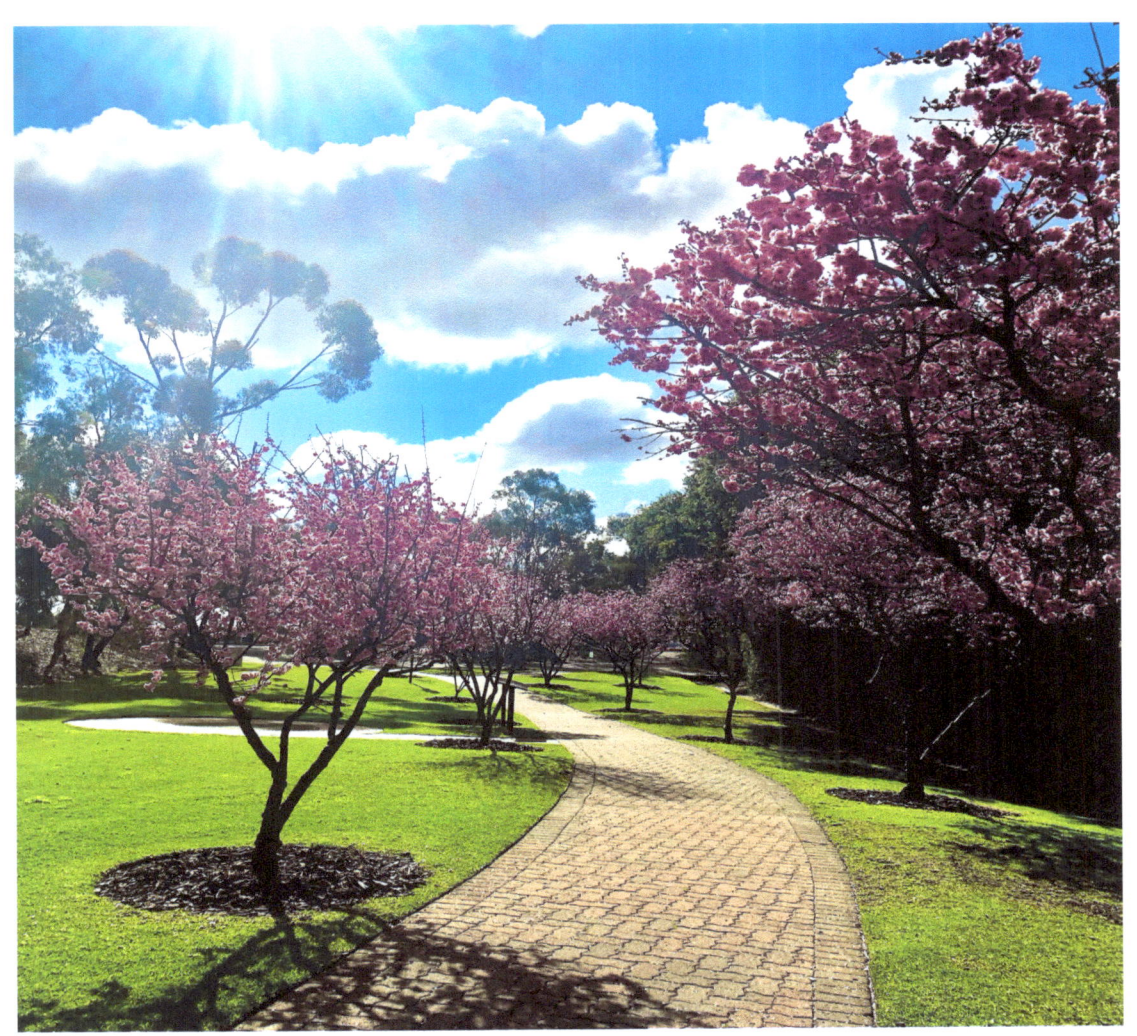
Stockade Botanical Park, South Australia

Embrace your day with:

Peace

Happiness

Love

Laughter

Understanding

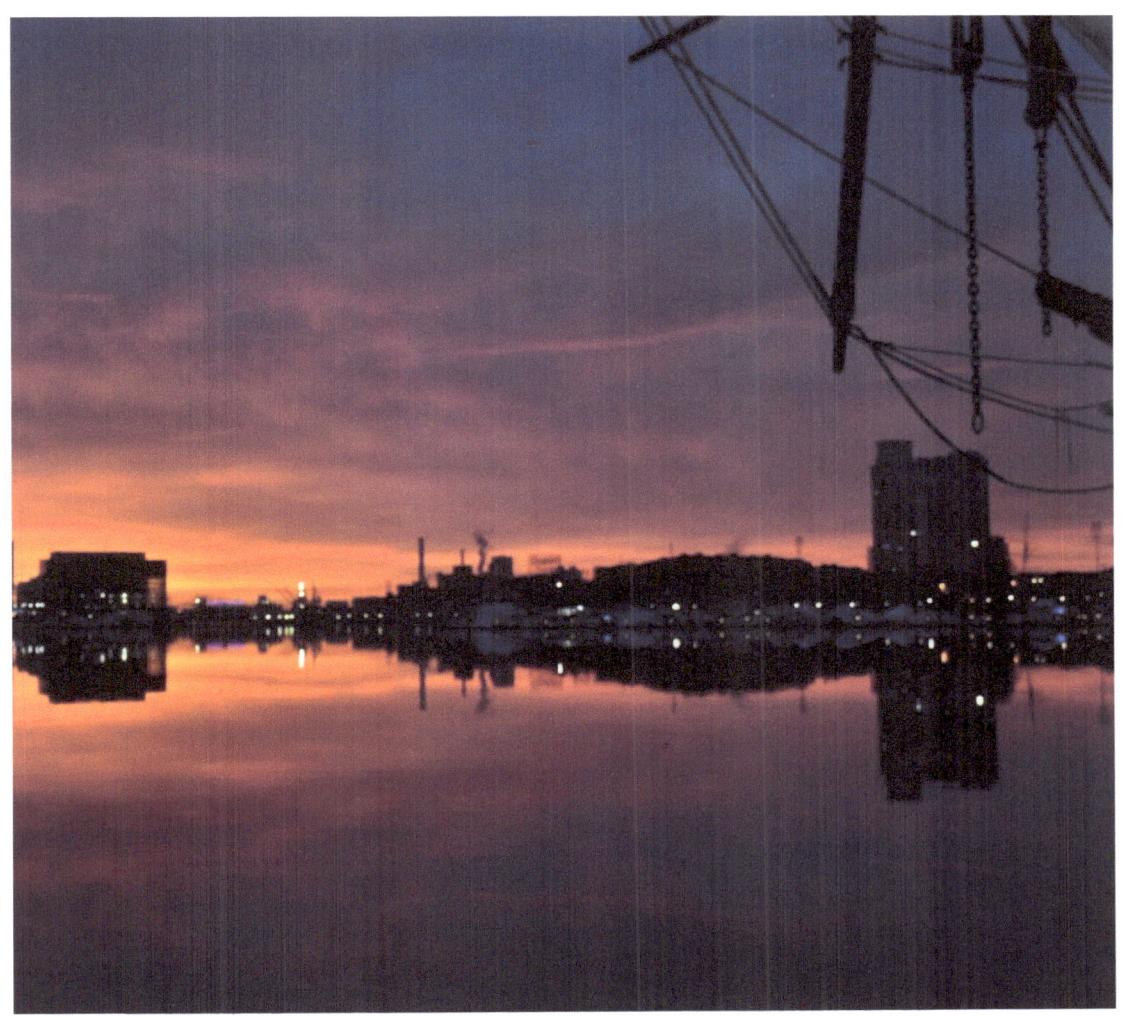

Inner Harbor, Baltimore, Maryland United States

Life is not defined…
It is not a paint
by numbers,
life is for living.

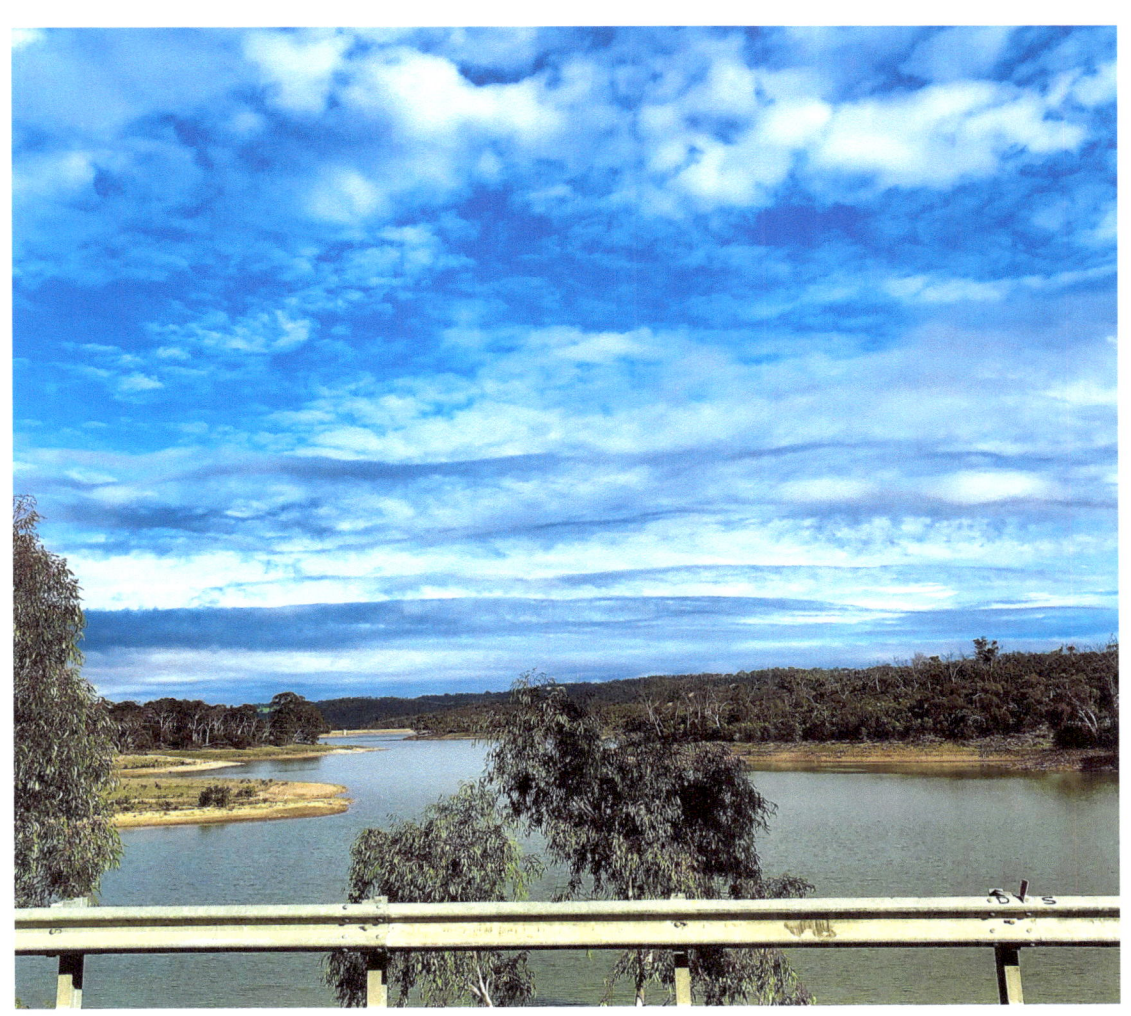

Adelaide Hills, South Australia

Your passion
Your love
Your heart
Your soul

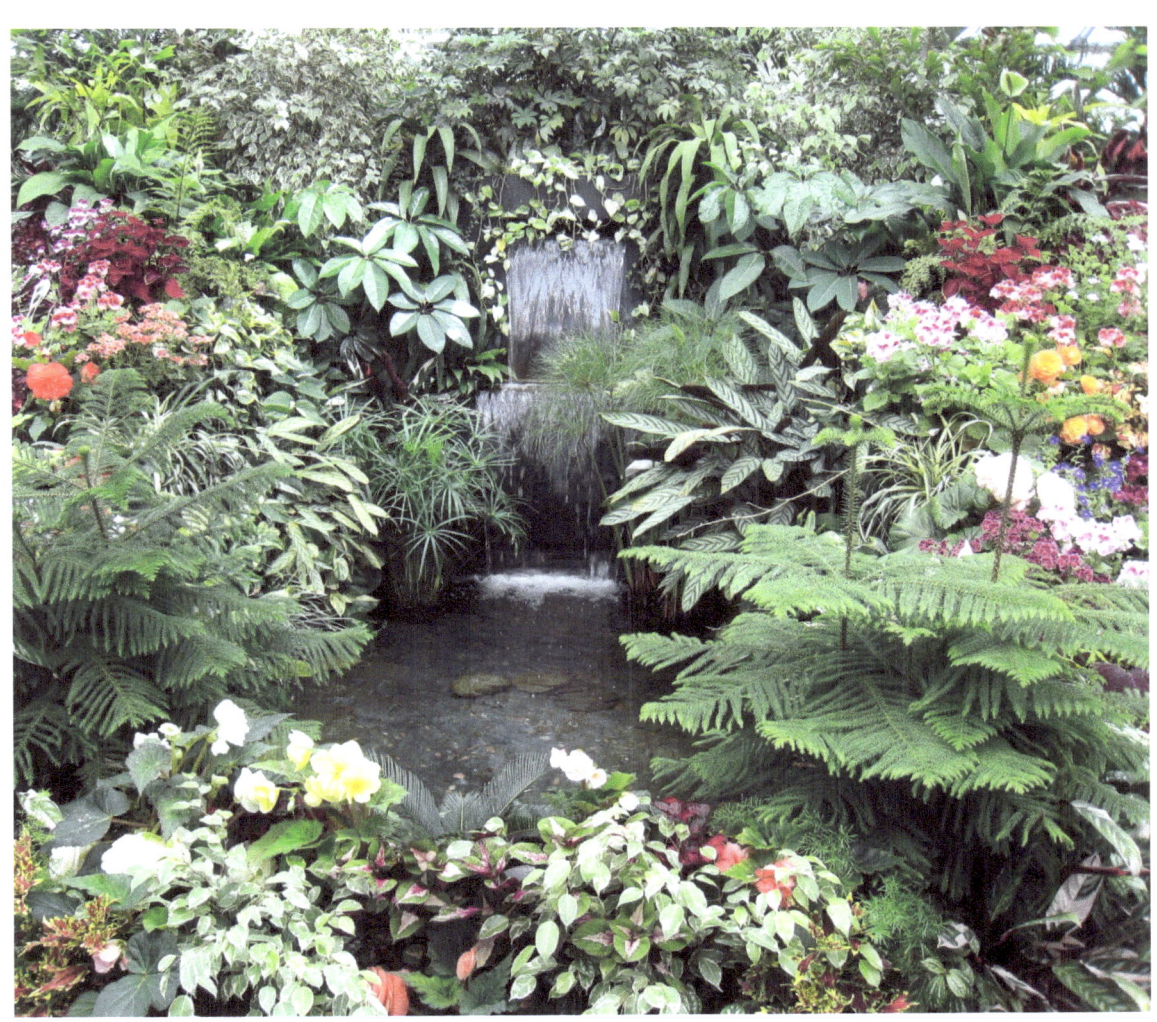

Keukenhof Gardens, Netherlands

When you find your
inner peace
everything else
falls in place.

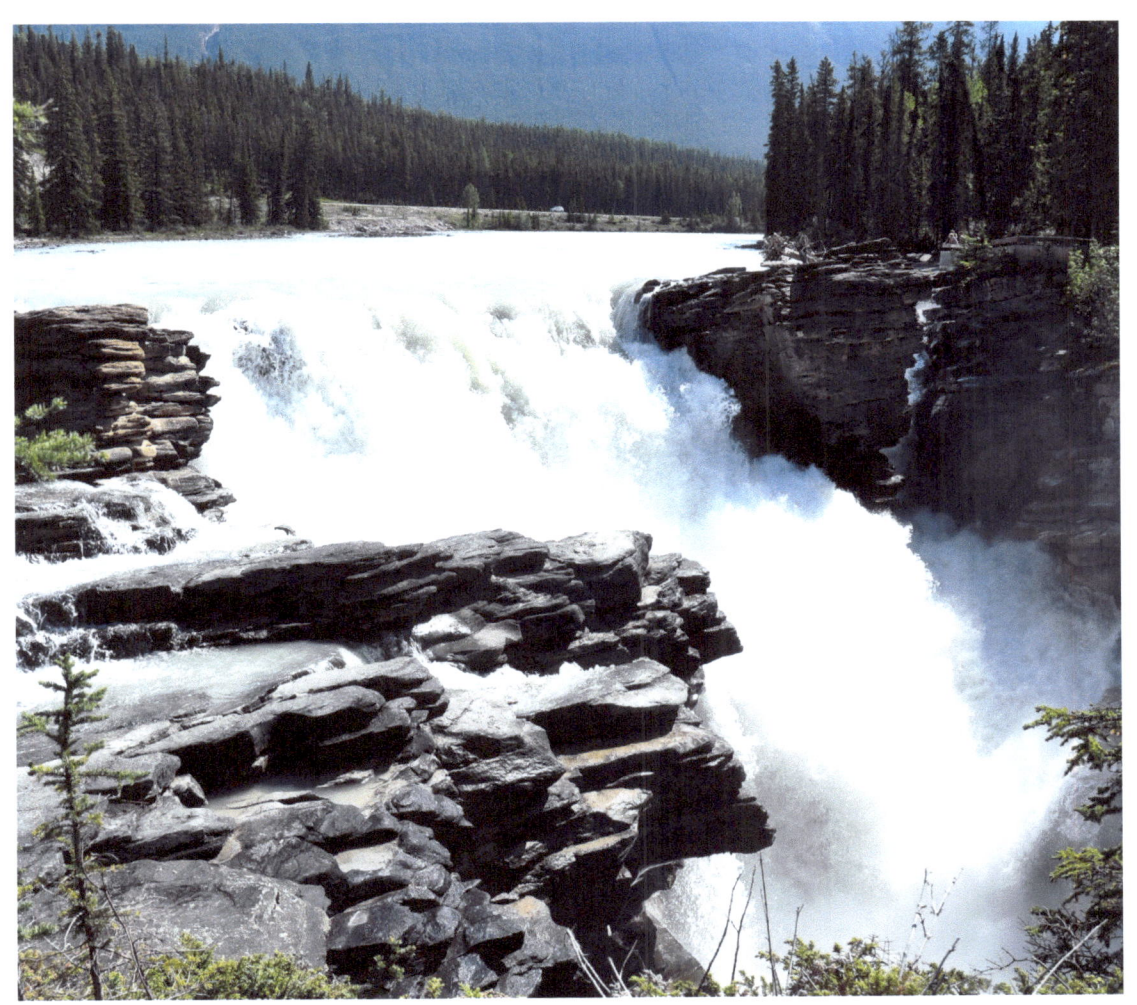

Waterfall, Canada

Smile …..
Daily

Laugh …..
Daily

Apologize …..
Let go of what you can't change

Keep going …..
Don't give up there is still time

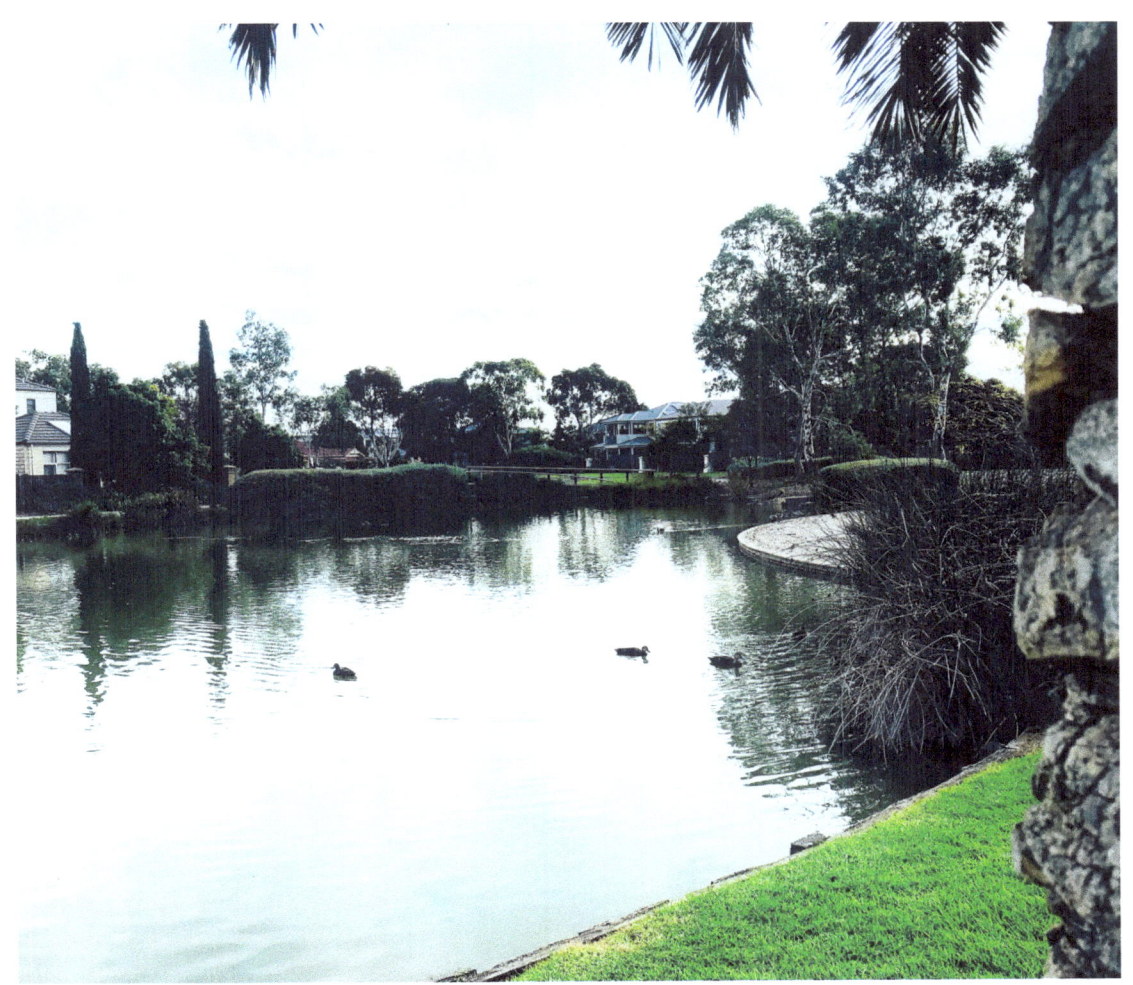

Mawson Lakes, South Australia

Friends are family we create, to surround ourselves with love and happiness.

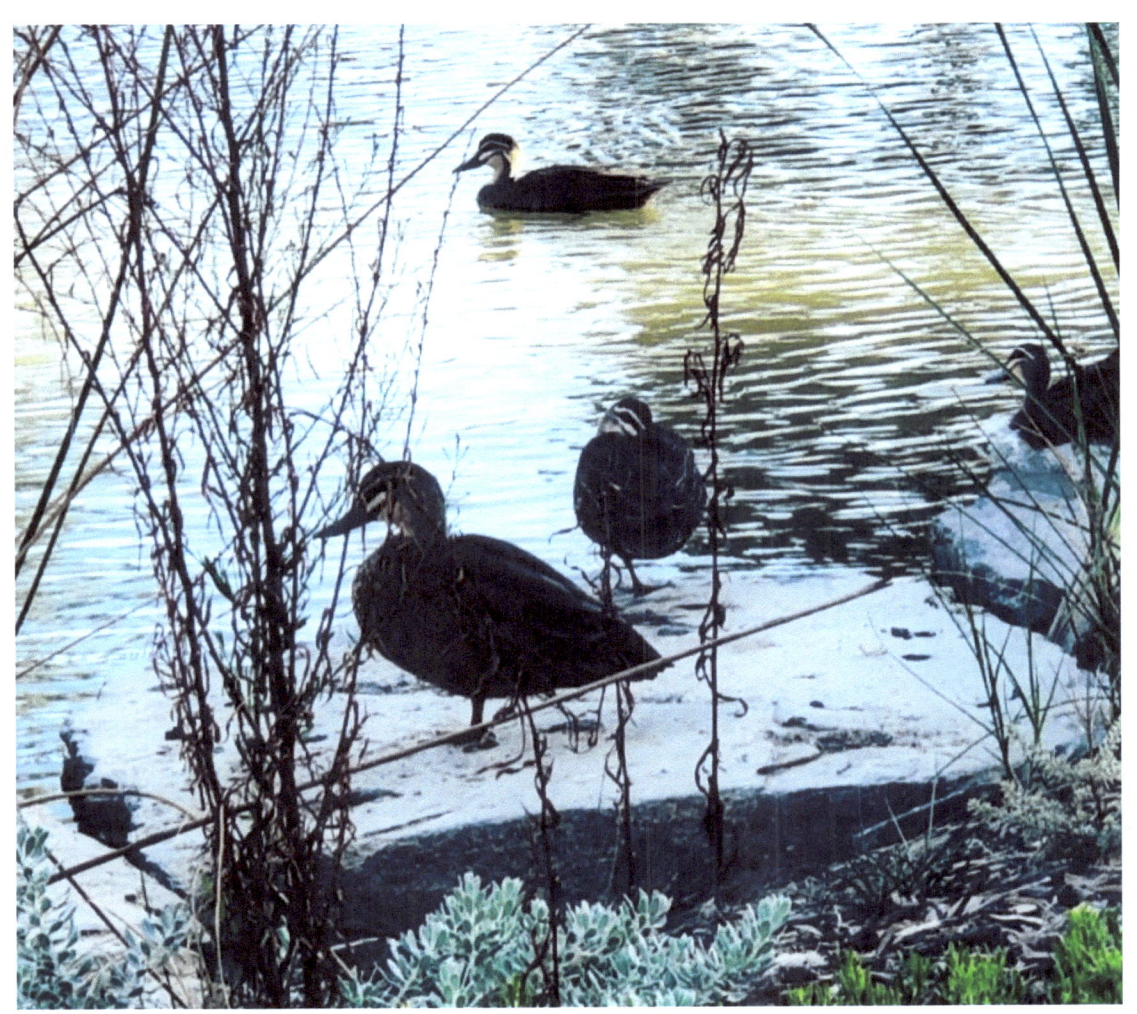

Mawson Lakes, South Australia

Smile & Laugh

Make your
sides hurt...

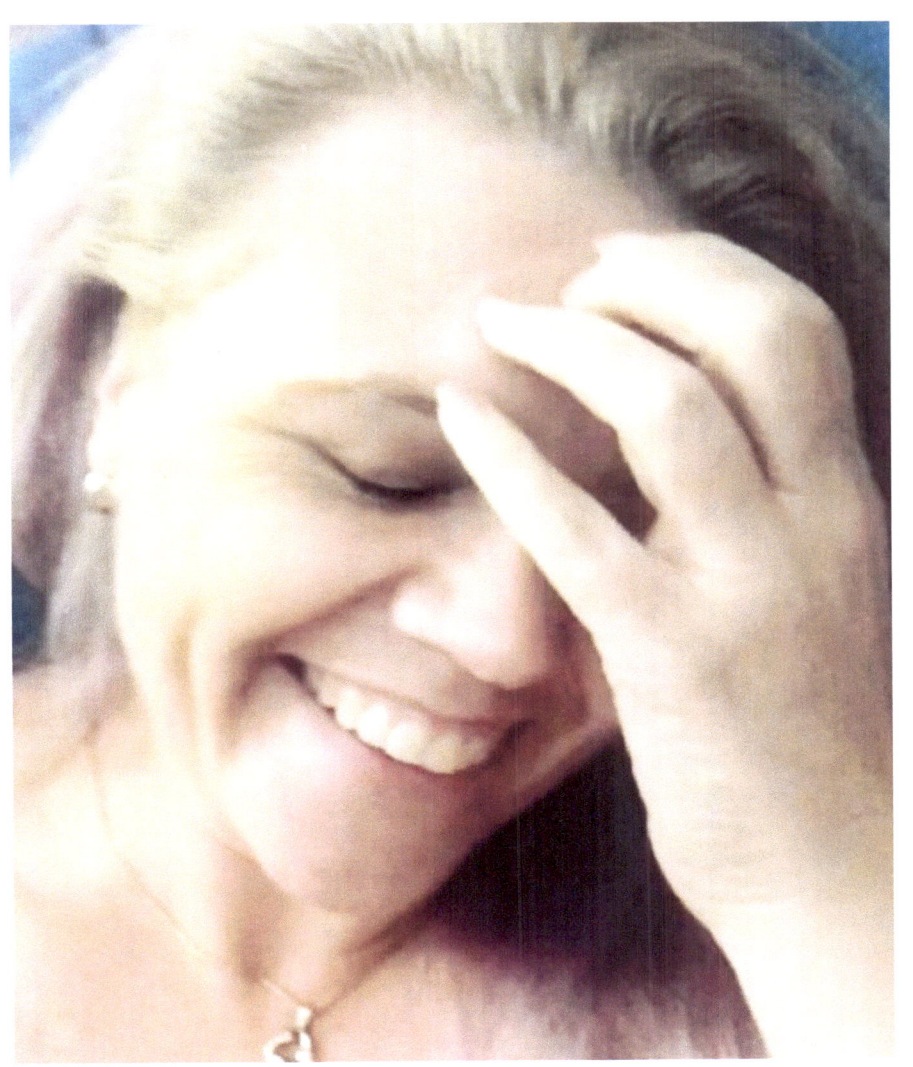

Life can be tough…

Rise above it all,
keep your head high,
focus on the blessings.

Smile and shine brighter.

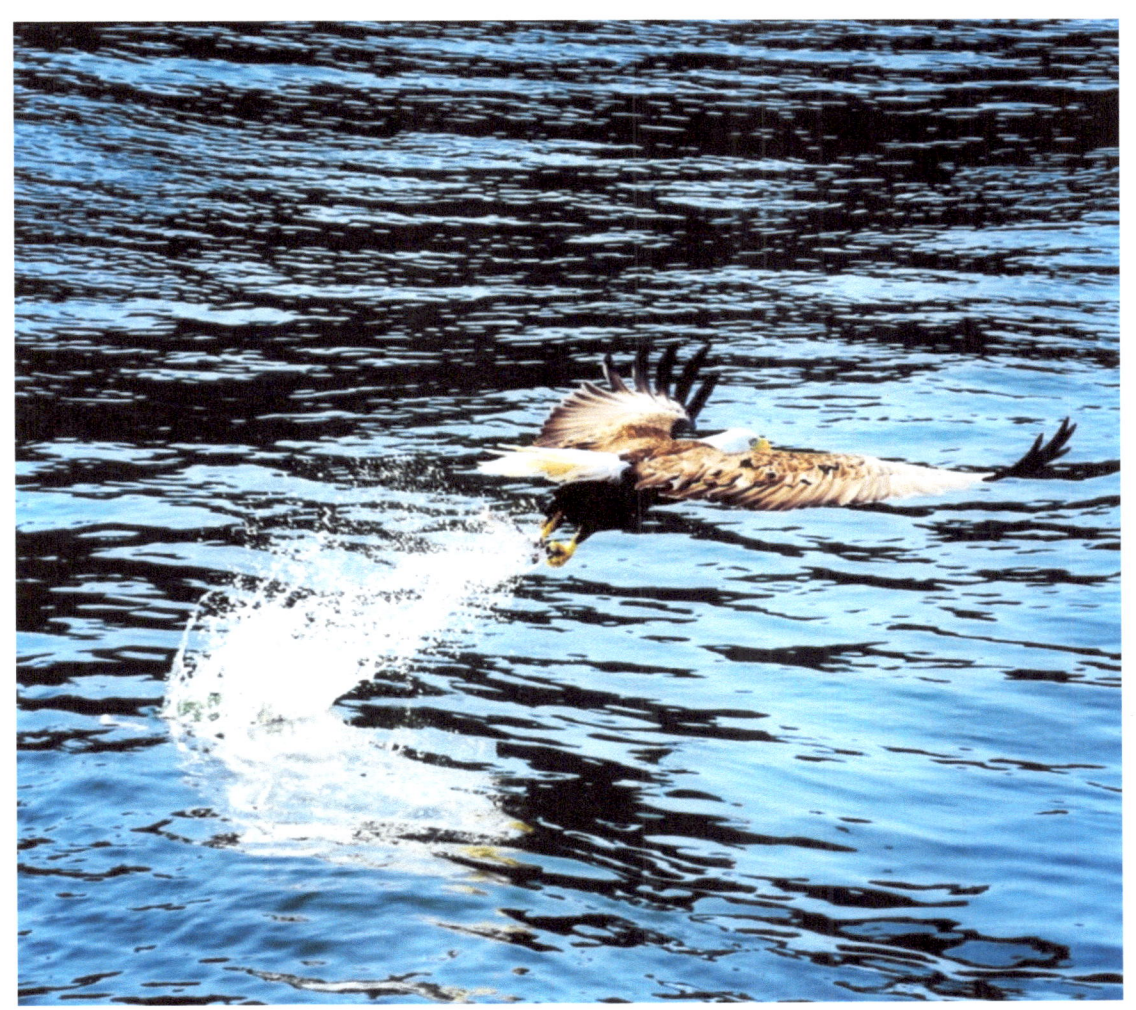

Eagle near Juneau, Alaska

It's there within

Your love is empowering

It touches in ways which can't be explained.

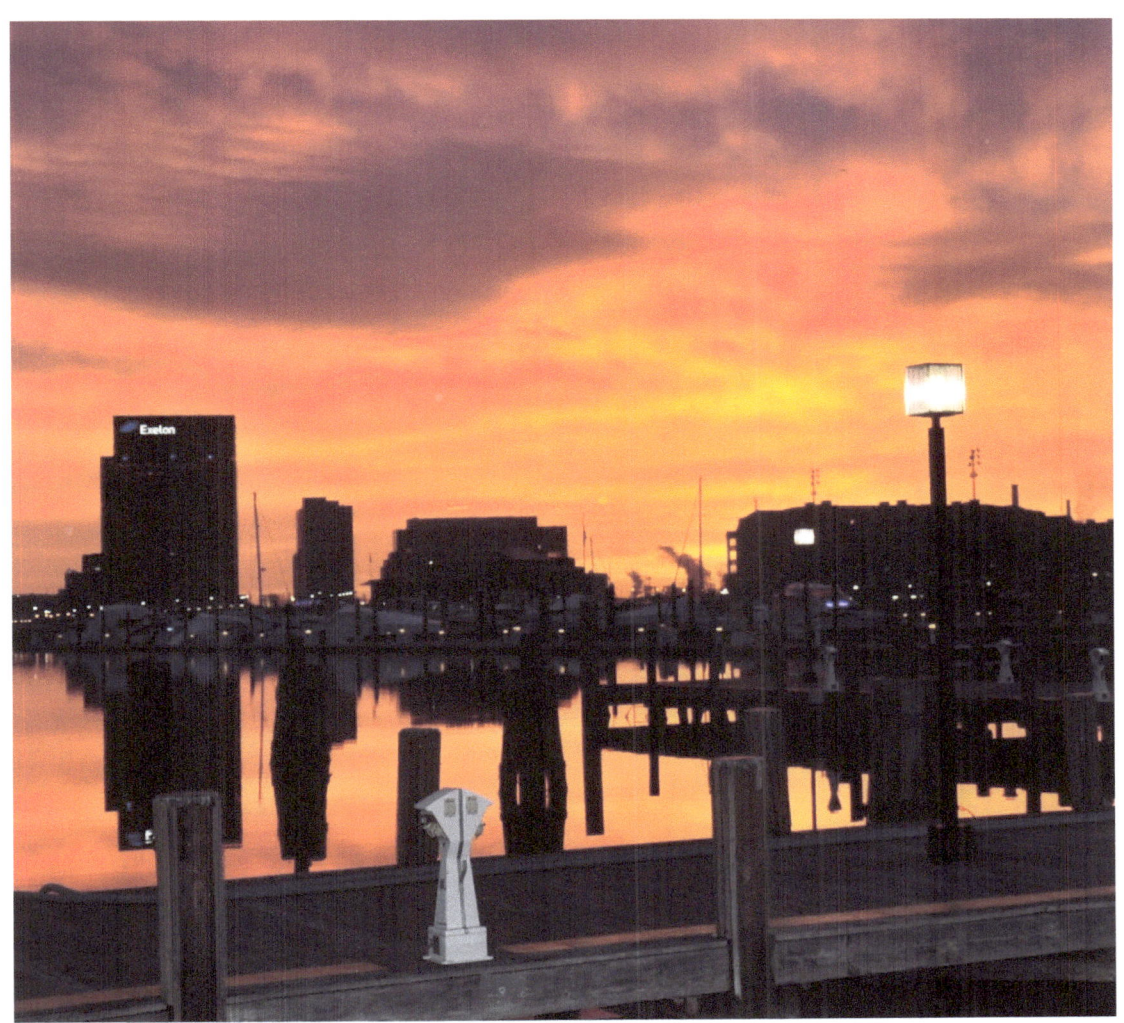

Inner Harbor, Baltimore, Maryland United States

Your words touched my heart
and your soul matched mine.
Although your eyes
were not seen,
they saw love from afar.
No matter where you are,
you will always be in my heart.

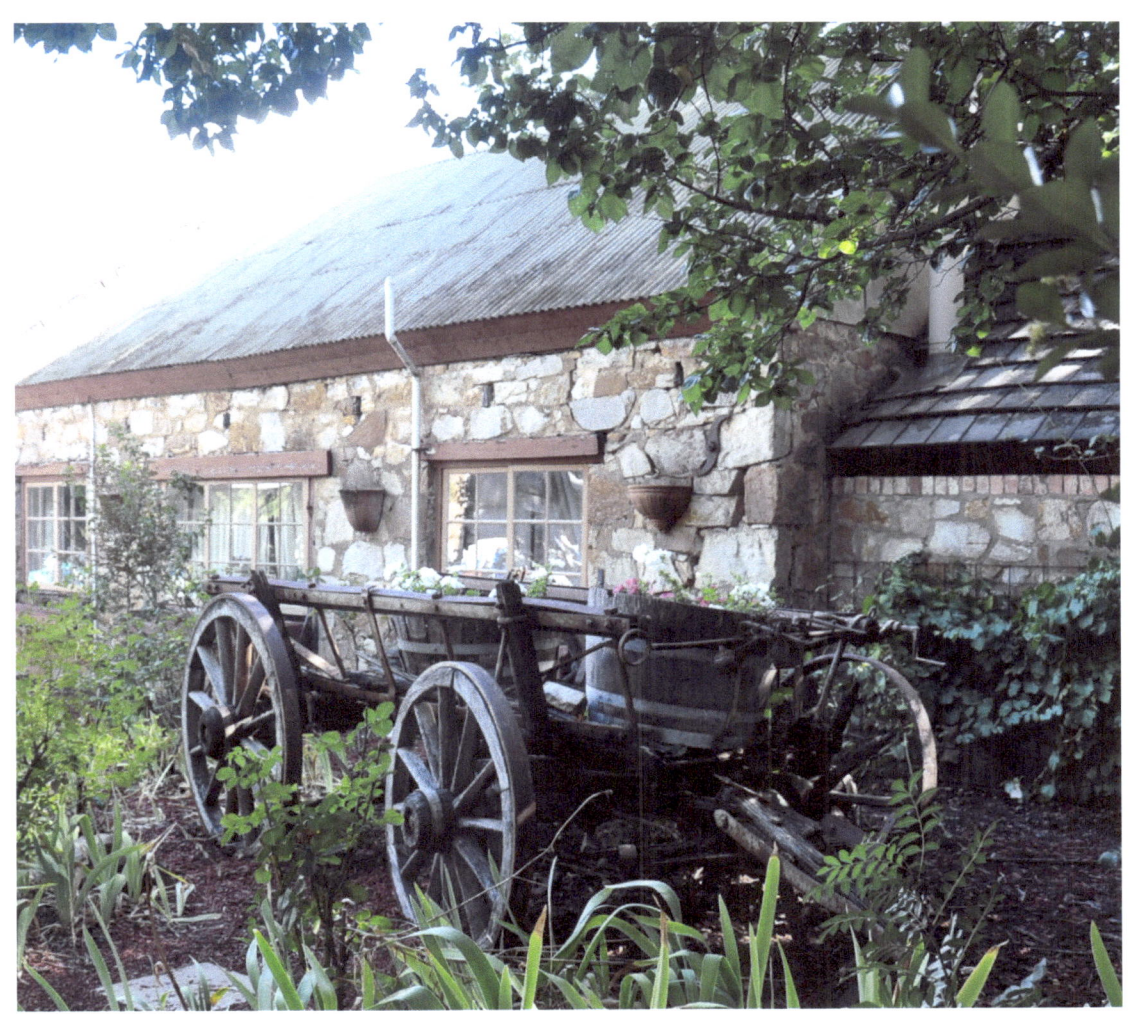

Hahndorf, South Australia

The sunset in your eyes intrigues me
The sunrise in your heart inspires me
The beating of your heart moves me
The tenderness of your words keep me
Two souls separated will always reunite
Distance may be far but closer than realised

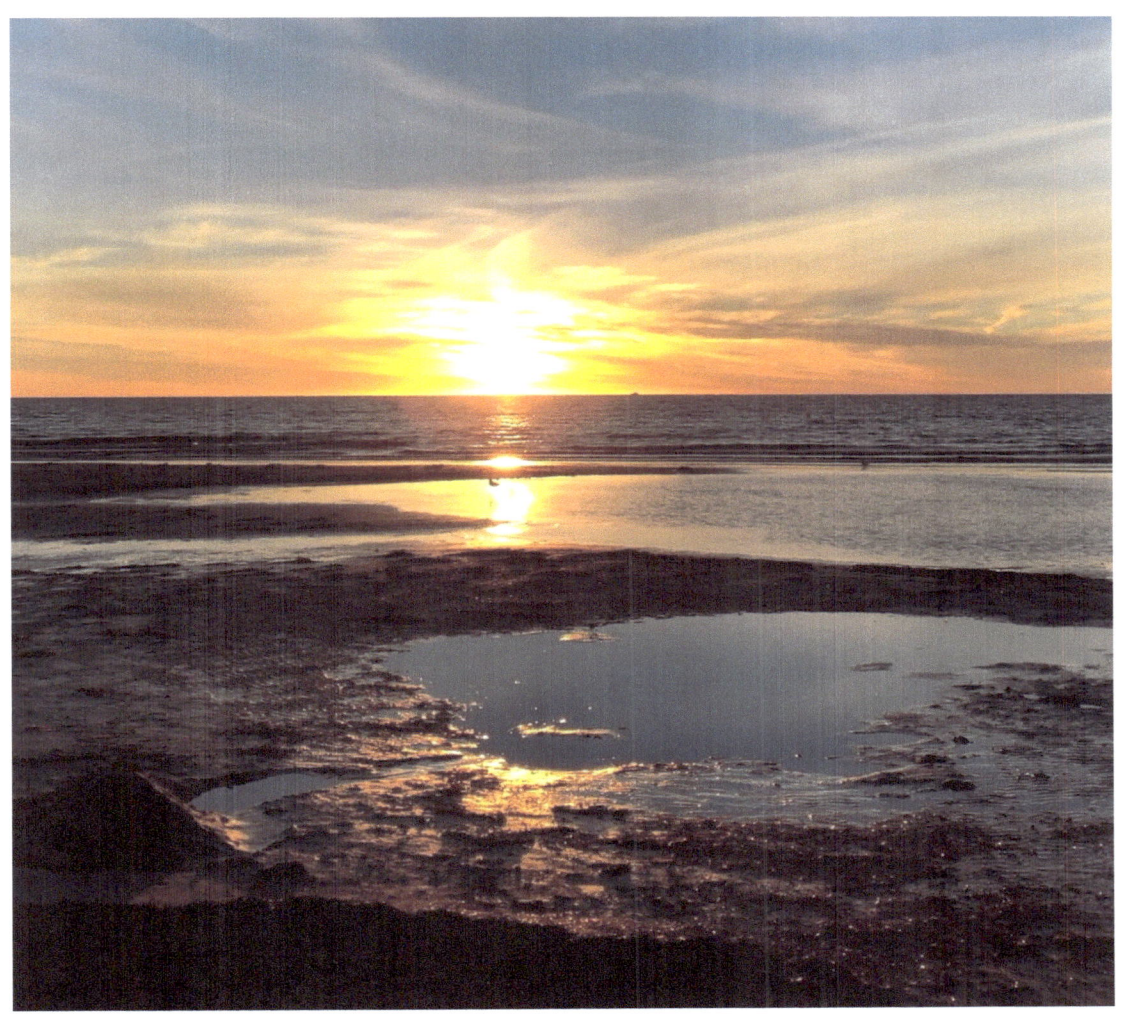
Semaphore Beach, South Australia

You do matter in life…
The smallest of things which may seem
unimportant actually touch others lives
without you realising it.
The smile you share, the joke you told, the hearts
you touched, or the song you sang.
It's the little things which make a big impact,
and are remembered when least expected.
Shine brightly and show love towards others.

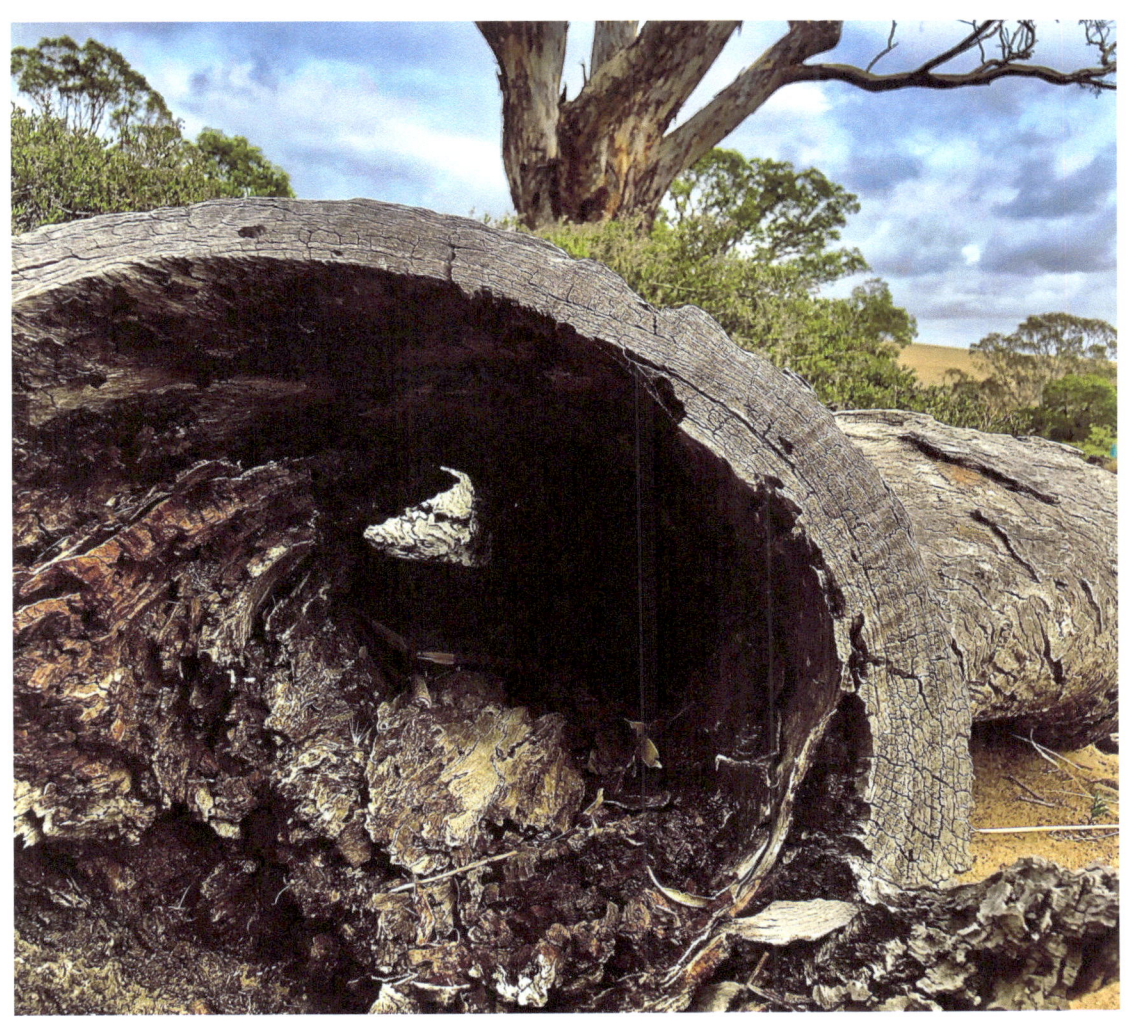

Lyndoch Lavender Farm, South Australia

Your support is valuable
Thank you for your love and Encouragement.
You are the light that shines
brighter everyday.
Your love flows deeply,
you are everything.
Never change...
You are amazing.

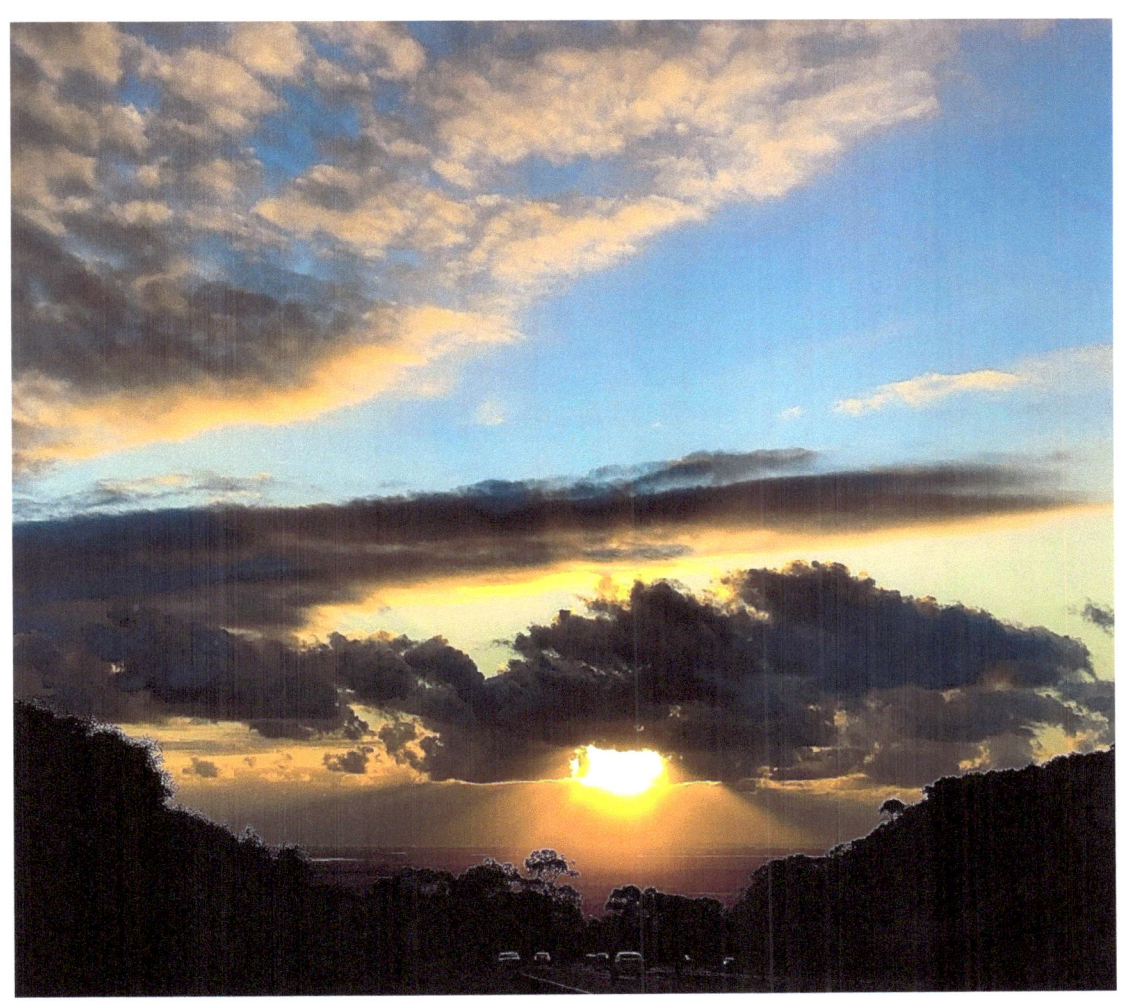
Winter Sun Set, Golden Way, South Australia

Today was perfect…
We had giggles
We had laughter
We had smiles
We had sunshine
We had each other

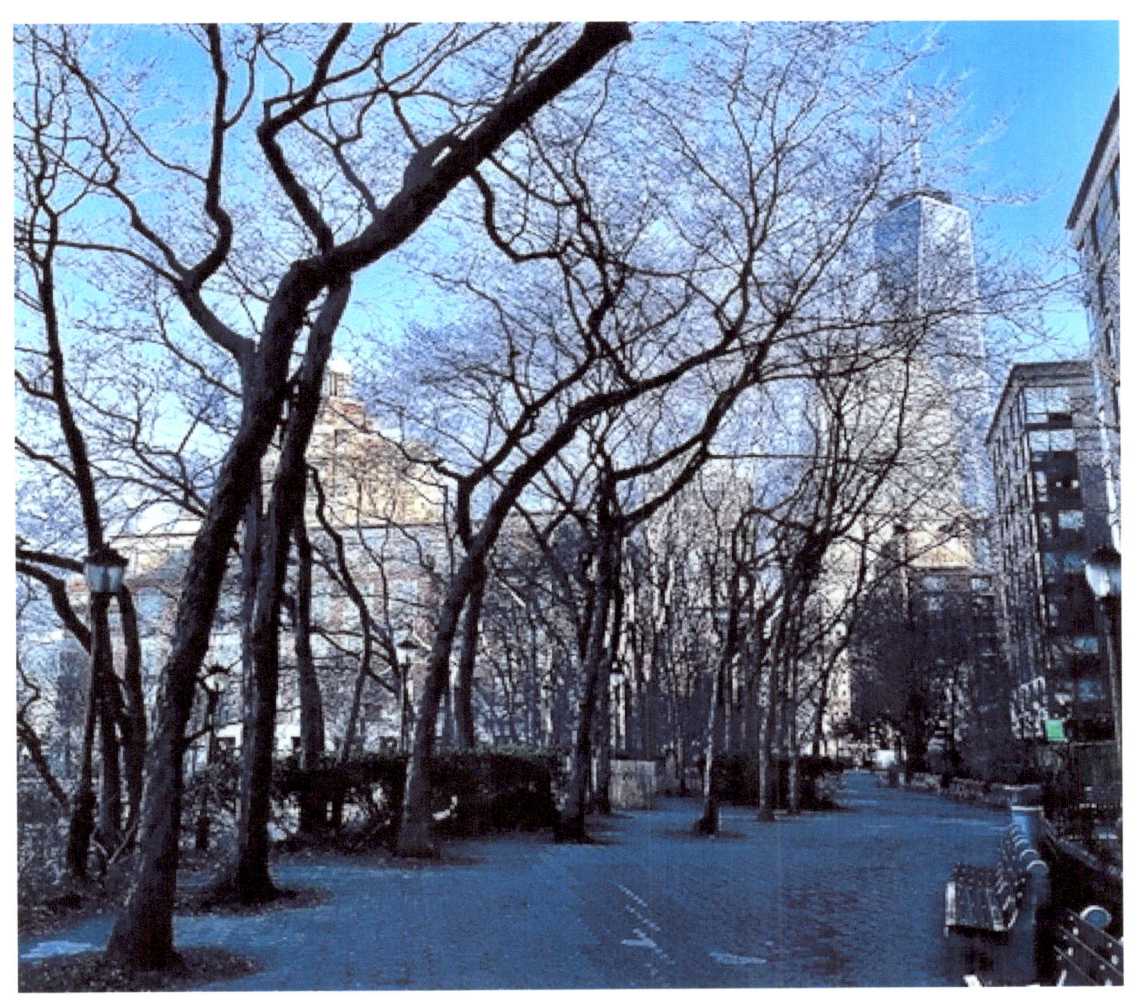

South Cove Park, New York United States

Your smile is like a
Chinese whisper,
It's passed on not
knowing the outcome.

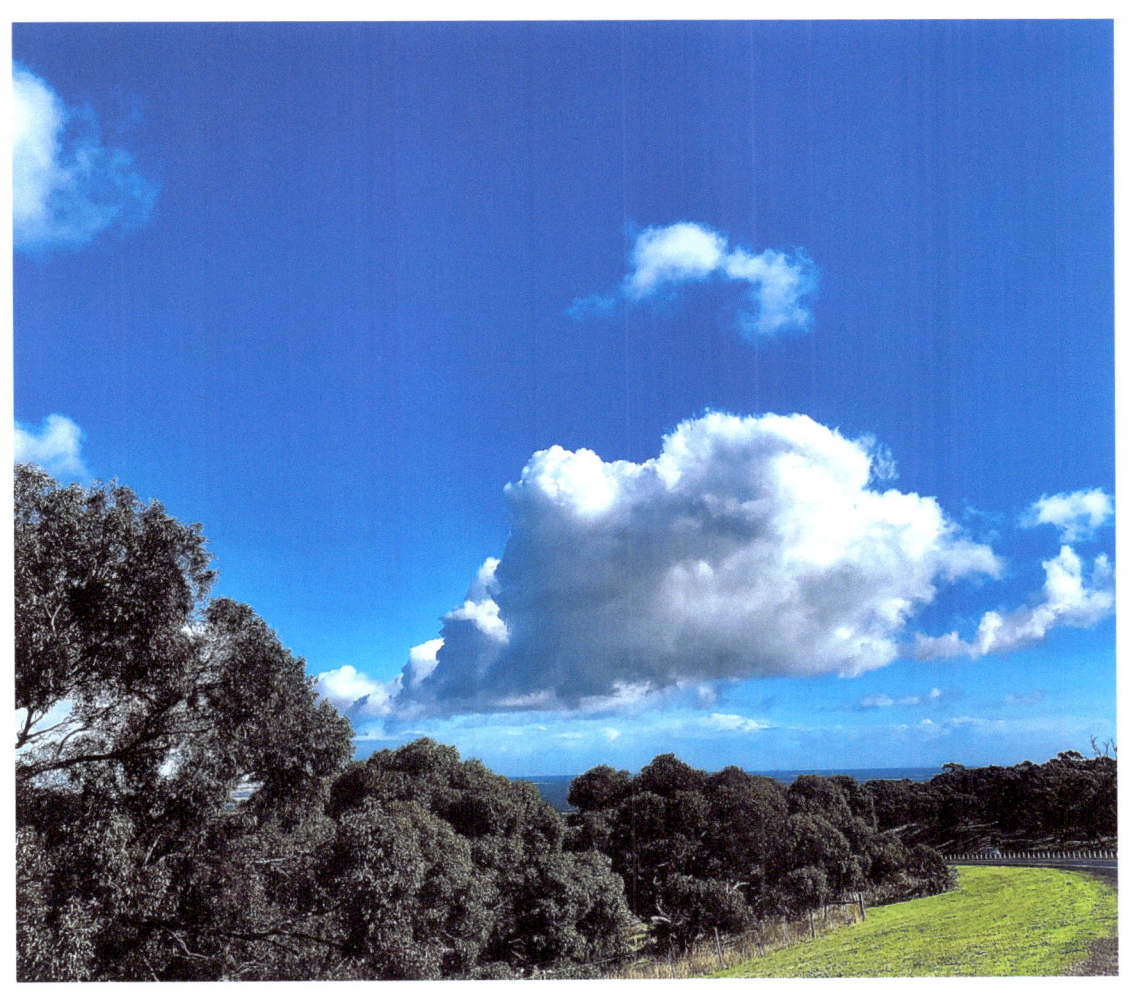

The Golden Way, Golden Grove South Australia

Like fast running water,
life will have obstacles.
Find your way,
stay positive and
follow your heart.

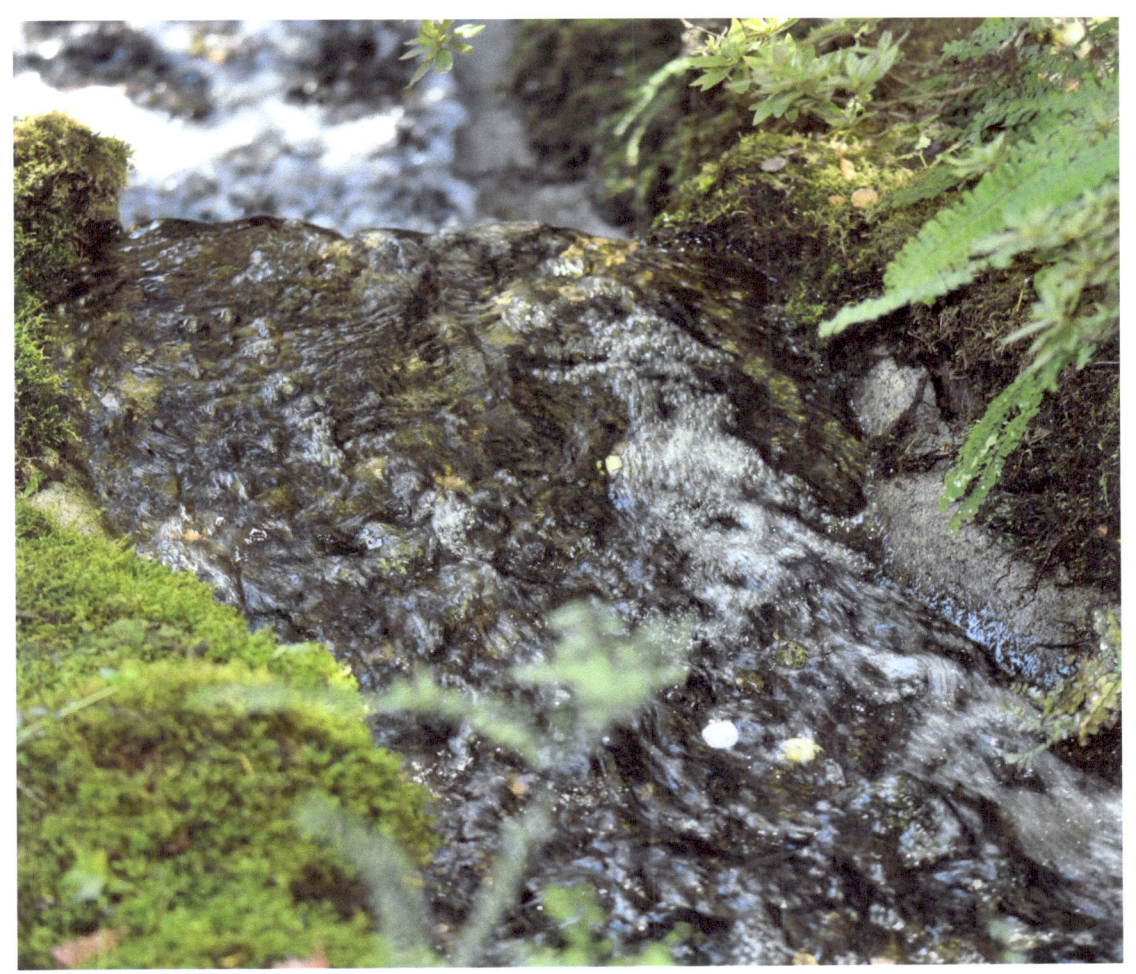

A stream in Skagway, Alaska

Your inner beauty
sparkles in your
EYES
and glows from your
SMILE.

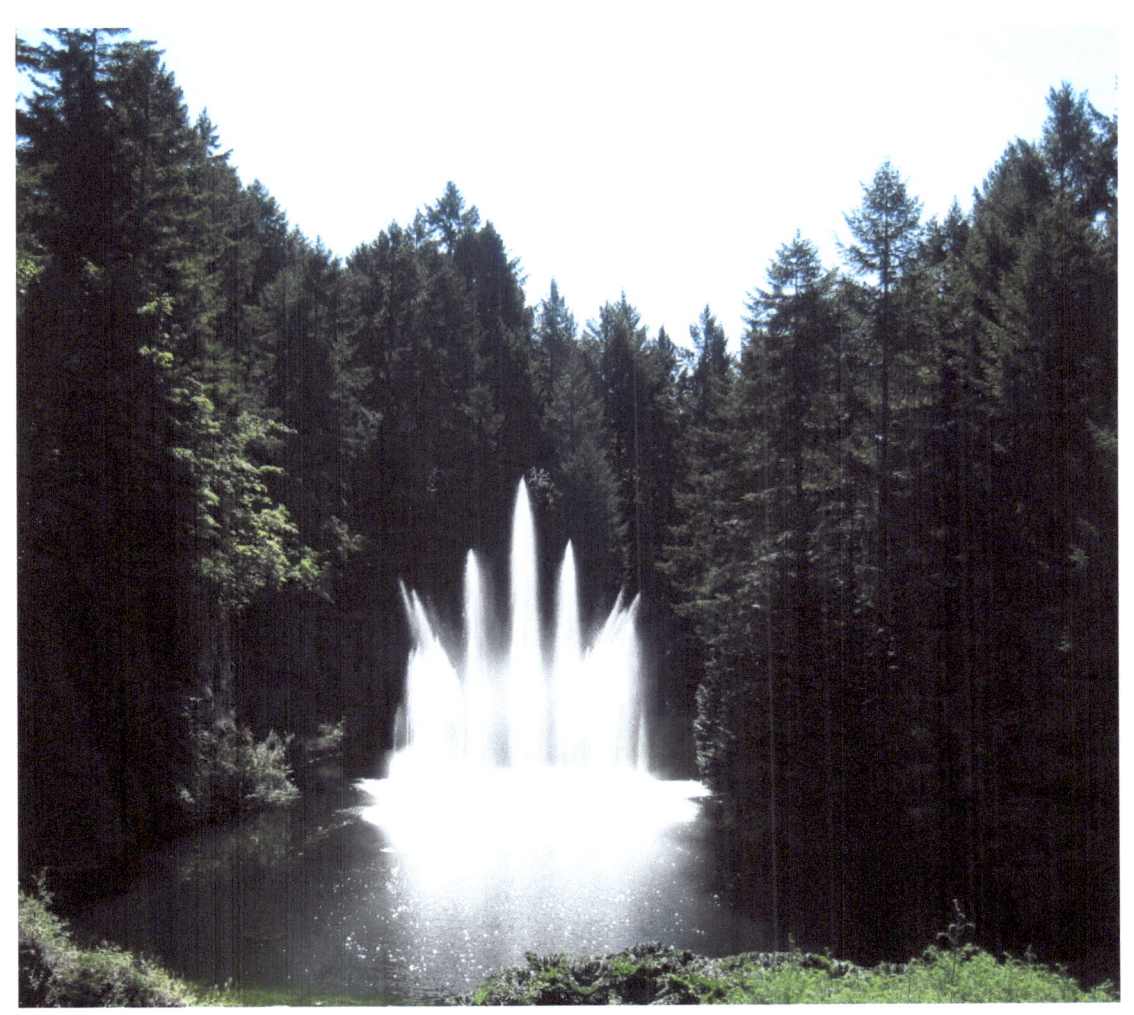

Butchart Gardens, Victoria Canada

When things seem tough,
keep going and remember
where you want to be…
Your focus and determination
will get you to the end.

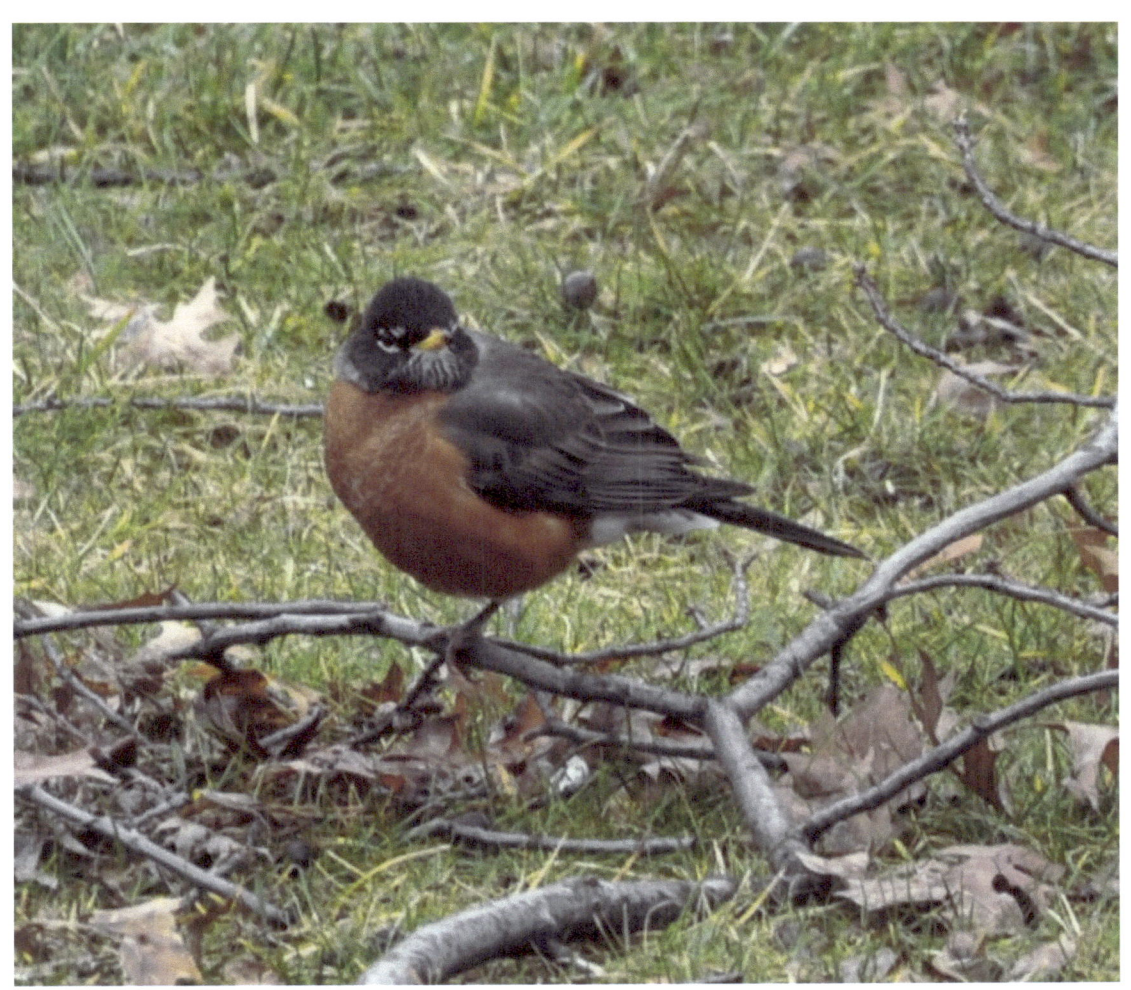

Central Park, New York United States

Love was found deep within,
happiness followed.
This in return radiated out
creating an abundance
to be shared.
Like a magnet, the love and
happiness was drawn back.

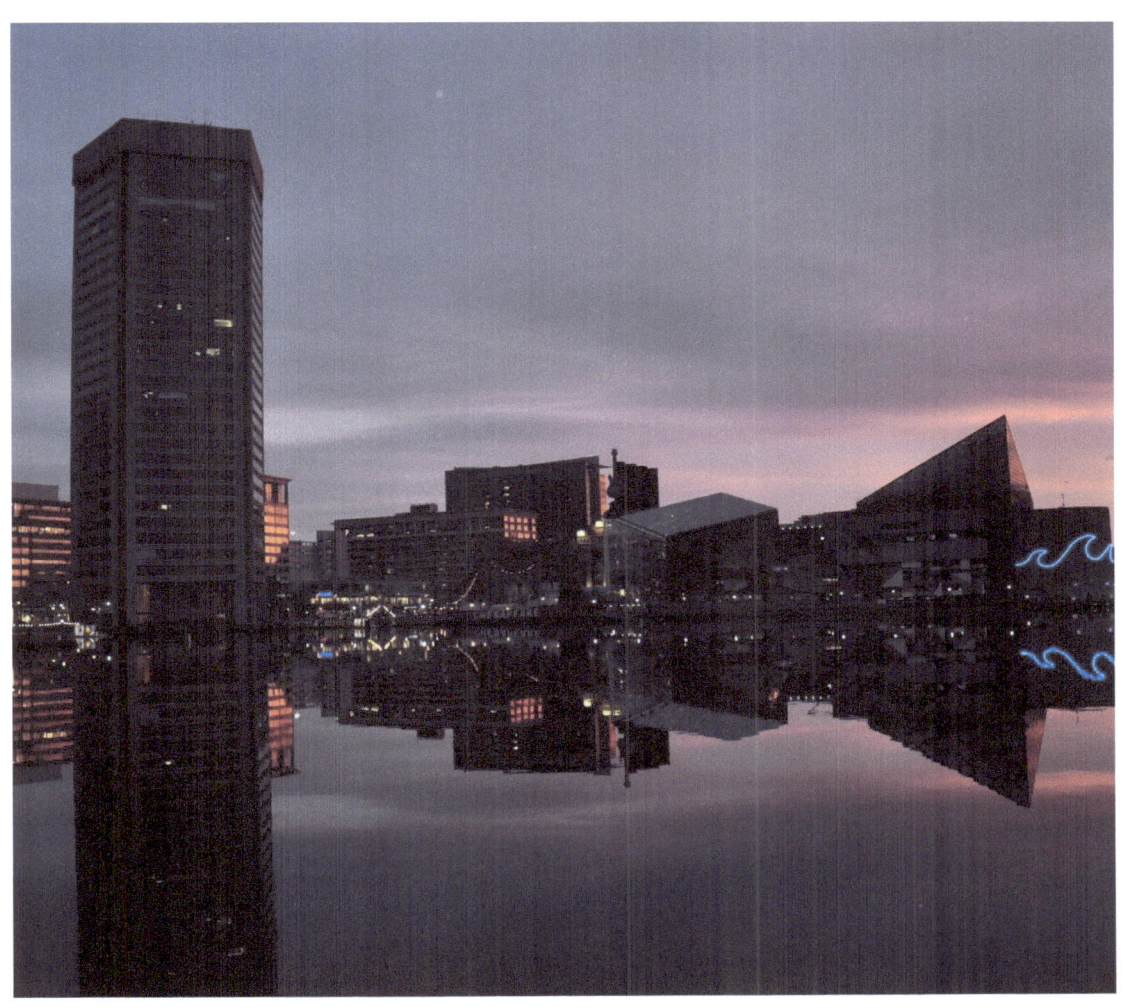
Inner Harbor, Baltimore, Maryland United States

You inspire me
You encourage me
You challenge me
YOU!
Complete me

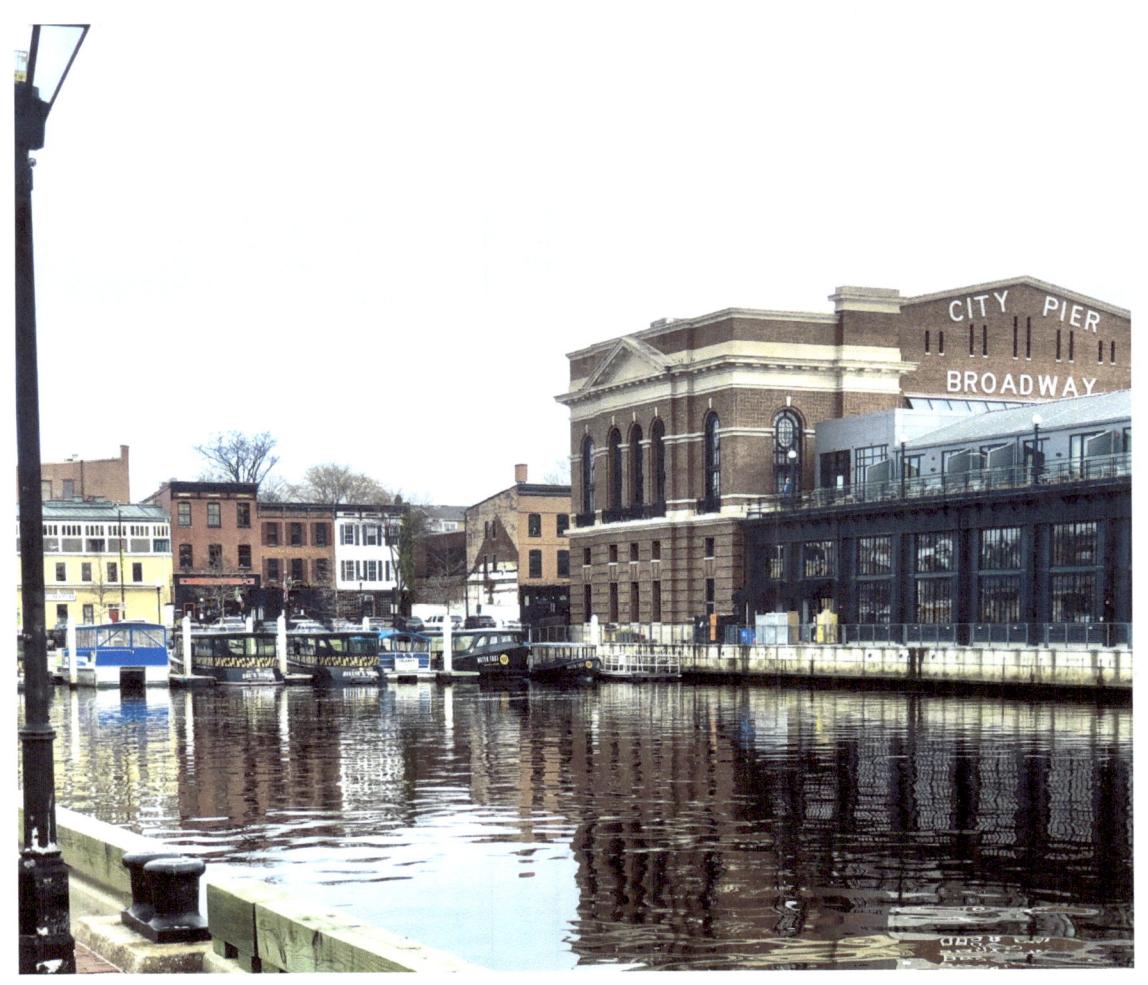

Fells Point, Baltimore, Maryland United States

Love, tenderness,
kindness, support,
happiness
and laughter…

You have it
You are it
Just be it.

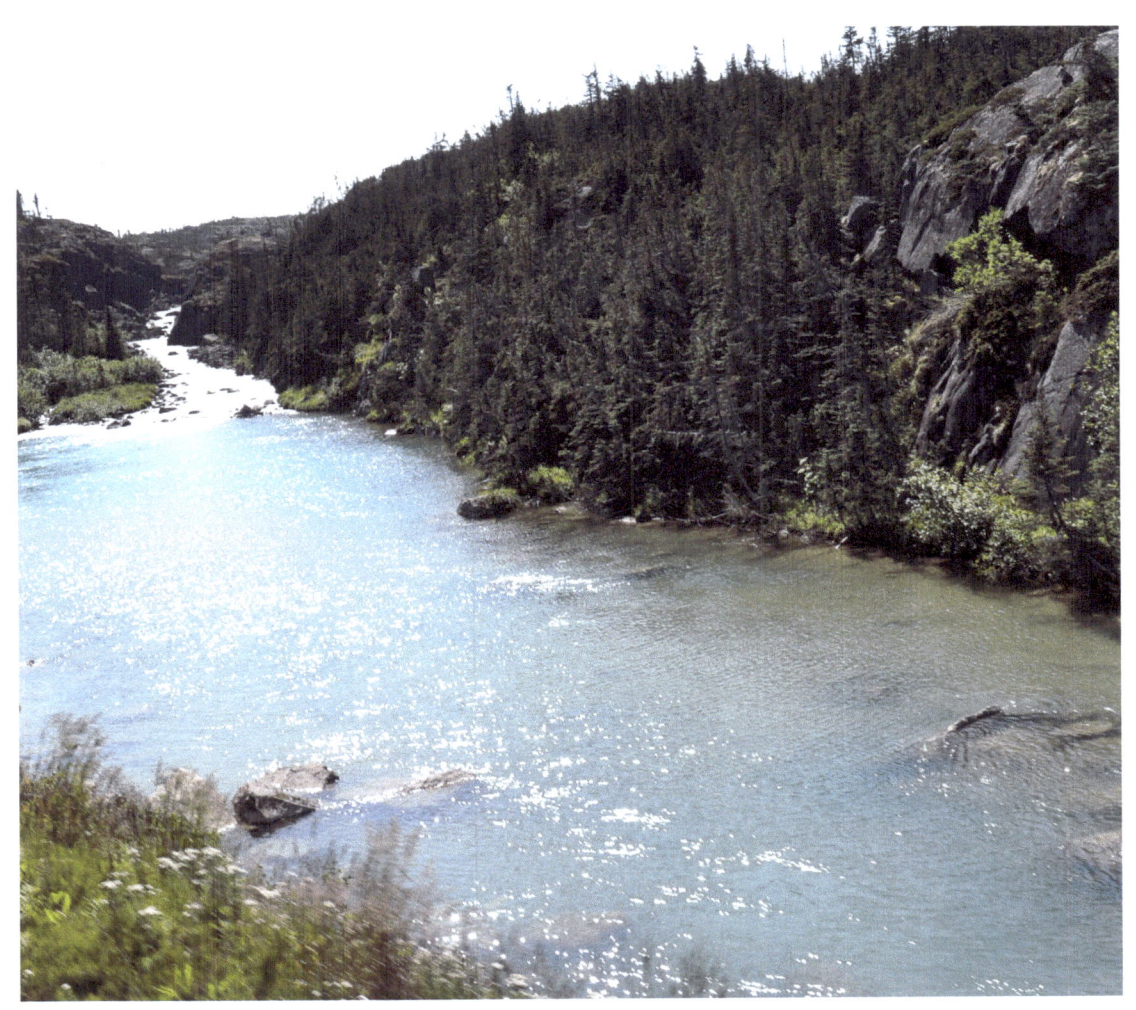
River in Alaska

Not everyone is
going to understand
your path…
It's Okay.

Do what is
important to you…
Stay Positive.

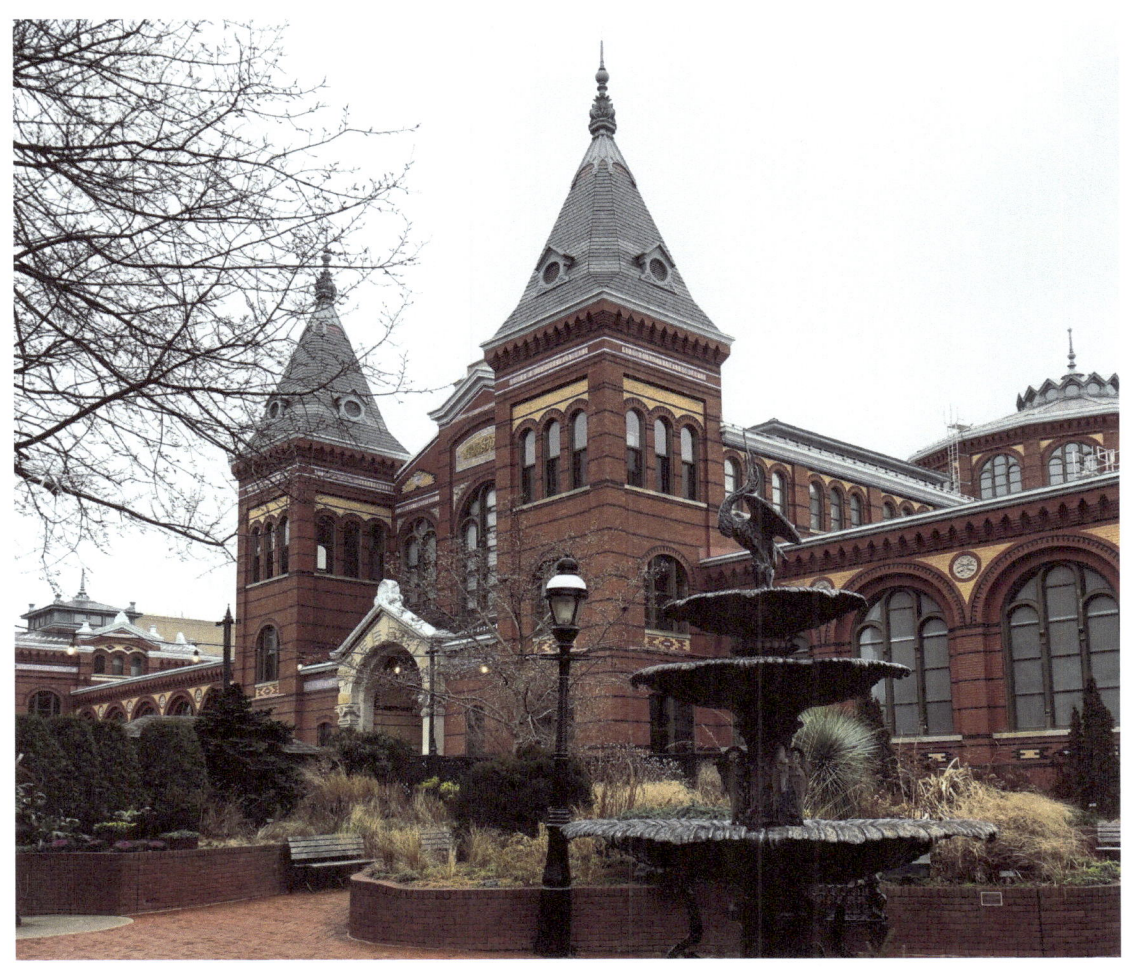

Mary Livingston Ripley Garden,
Washington DC, United States

Don't let the shadows
cast darkness in life,
Let the light shine bright
guiding you along the way.

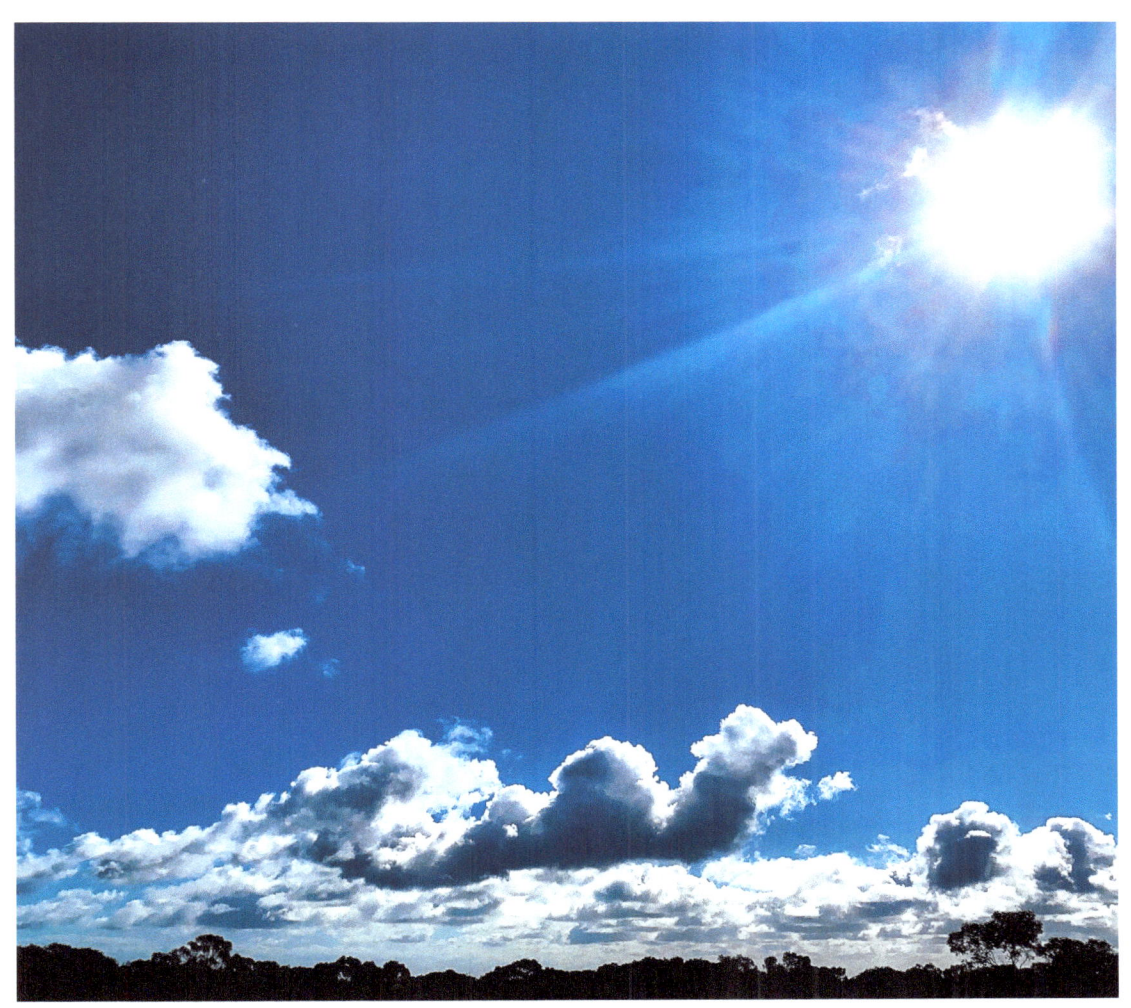

Winter Sun, South Australia

Thank you for purchasing this book.

May you find inspiration,
feel love and find happiness.
May your path be rewarding
and stimulating.

Keep smiling and
stay blessed ….

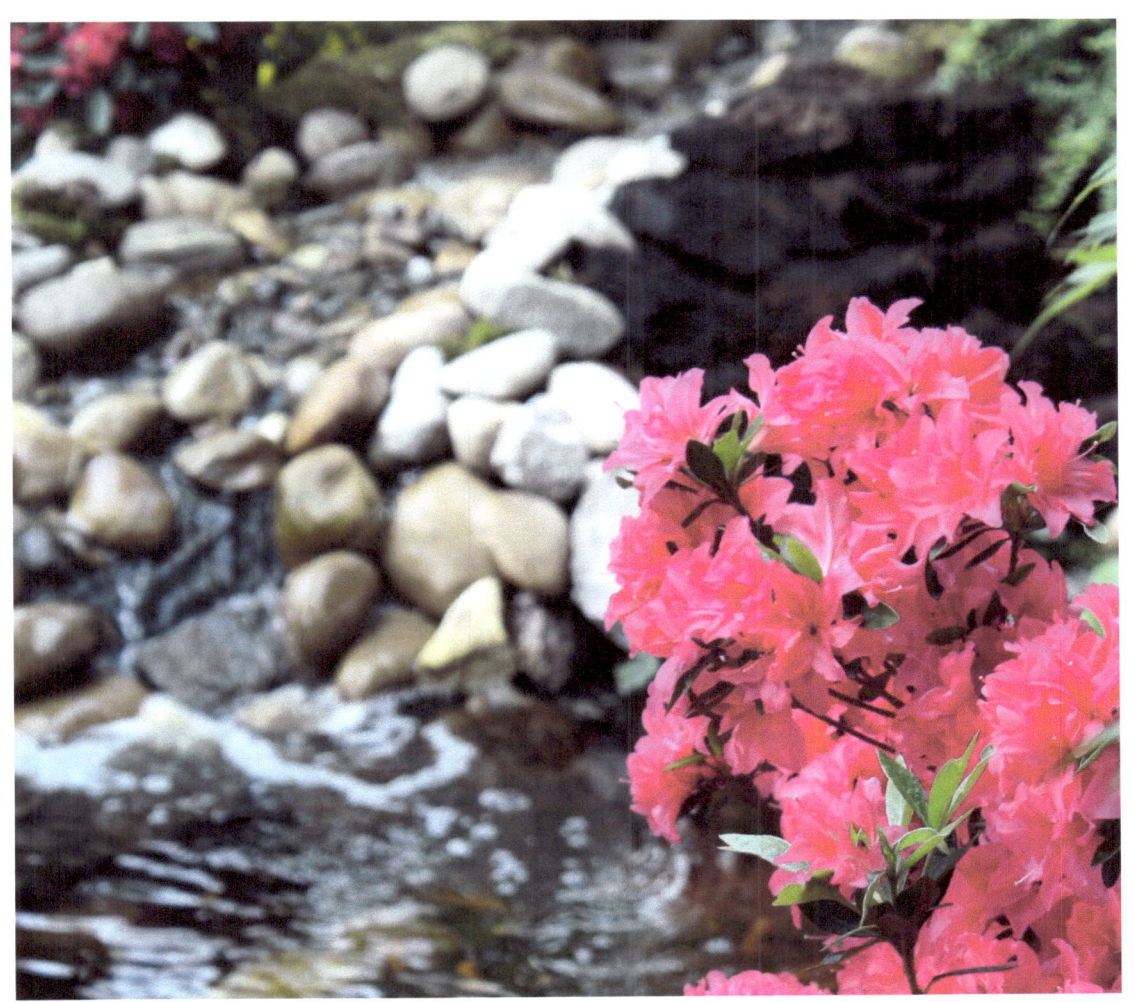

Keukenhof Gardens, Netherlands

www.ingramcontent.com/pod-product-compliance
Lightning Source LLC
Chambersburg PA
CBHW051209220526
45473CB00003B/961